True to Poetry in my Fashion

Peter Jeffery OAM

regime
books

True to Poetry in my Fashion
by Peter Jeffery

Published by Regime Books in Australia, 2015.
267 William Street, Perth.
www.regimebooks.com.au
www.twitter.com/regimebooks
www.instagram.com/regimebooks

Cover design: Nathan Hondros
Cover image: © 2015 Guido Nigro

ISBN 978-0-9874821-6-7

Dedication

This book is dedicated to Professor Vijay Mishra for his kind support in making Murdoch University realise that I was a poet of some national import and a cultural activist and hence worthy of promotion to Senior Lecturer after I had brooded like Corialanus for some twelve years because of a broken promise that I would be give that status after my first year of transfer from WAIT to Murdoch.

CONTENTS

Foreword

Consider those moments in art history when workmen, stripping a wall of its surface, reveal a vivid fresco long painted over and forgotten. I propose this idea as a kind of origin-myth for a West Australian literature. A myth is not a falsehood. It is a useful starting point for discussing an emerging awareness of the existence of a unique body of writing about the strangely peaceful and forbidding State of Western Australia. The white-washed wall is the state's dreadful capacity to ignore and forget; the vivid fresco is the literature; and the workmen, those students who strive to cultivate a creative and intellectual life in a state unaccustomed to serious self-examination.

The poems in this volume represent just a fraction of the work of Peter Jeffery, one of our most unjustly neglected writers. Jeffery was part of a generation of poets, playwrights and novelists that emerged out of the shadows of Katharine Susannah Pritchard and Randolph Stow in the decades immediately following World War 2, and has maintained a steady level of productivity right up to the present day. His work is of inestimable aesthetic and historical value because it documents the trends and movements, the fashions and controversies that have rolled through West Australian writing for over half a century.

There are numerous reasons why Peter's work hasn't attained the prominence of some of his contemporaries. I hope he'll forgive me when I say that he himself has been partly to blame. Like so many other writers and artists in this city, I knew Peter first as a lecturer at Murdoch University, later as a tireless mentor and hardworking activist on the boards of various funding bodies. Only slowly over the years, have I come to realise what a serious writer he is and how hard it must be, putting his own work aside to help others.

Perhaps another reason for the neglect is that his is an entirely metropolitan voice, middle class, university educated and well-travelled. Its poetics are hard-wired in Anglo-American modernism, rigorously adapted to local conditions. In a publishing culture that for so long has sought the exotic colour of the rural and remote, Peter's work seemed perhaps too internationalist, too far ahead in the world to satisfy the market-driven preoccupations of isolation.

With the publication of these poems another part of that fresco which is West Australian literature has come to light. It is a selection that marks, with the eye and ear of a restless and disenchanted intellect, the ambiguity of cultural life in Perth and Western Australia over the last sixty years. It seeks, in a language of dishevelled beauty and aching sensuality to make forms out of the savage light and the introverted society in thrall to it. In a state accustomed to the toil of sleepwalkers, this is the poetry of a mind that never sleeps, always probes and searches for any stirrings of life.

Chris Palazzolo
Queens Park, 2015

Introduction

During the 2014 *WAPI Poetry Festival* I attended a panel that tried to determine what poetry was. I ventured the Arnold dictum, 'The best possible words in the best possible order'. Someone countered, 'Who determines "best"?' I moved away from my initial elitist proposition and possible arrogance to say I understood that poetry came from the word 'poesis' which broadly means 'pattern making' with words and even sounds as a medium. In that case anyone who played with words and generated a pattern could call that creation 'poetry'.

However one would need a reciprocal agreement for it to be acknowledged as such even if it was only a single person that concurred. Hence the countless schools of poetry in contention such as the dominant rhymed metrical form versus 'free verse' and lately with rap performed verbal articulations or from the introduction of print pagination and calligrams. One needs a constituency of two to generate a poetry of sorts, no matter how idiosyncratic or seemingly bizarre the patterning is or what other readers might think.

In inviting my *Regime* editorial colleague Chris Palazzolo to run through and select a collection of poems from an output of some 62 years I have found my constituency, albeit of two, and hopefully many, many more. Initially I had intended to publish all my poetic endeavours thus creating a timeline or parallel universe of my poetry and my life as a family memoir, but one wonders if people really read telephone book volumes of poetry right through. Hence the chronological basis of this book, not always precisely accurate with many generous 'circas' that disregards thematic consistencies and my valuation of and regard for the quality of each poem, but as my title states I have been *True to Poetry in my Fashion*.

In the vein of democratic constituencies with access to all, I point to a crude miniature unglazed maquette which cost less than a dollar that I chose in preference to say a huge vase of porcelain which would make an interior decorator happy for its grand elegance and obvious expensiveness. We had stopped at a roadside ceramic factory on our way to Halong Bay and the solely commissioned junk for the day, and my two wealthy hosts offered me anything in the factory as a souvenir. They were surprised by my choice, even though it now has pride of place on my mantelpiece alongside two stones from Anzac Cove.

I had to explain to them that this group of three men around a table with wine cups in hand were like the free and spirited exchange of poets in the give and take of presenting their personal poems each to the other. For me then they are the joy of poetry, the sharing of each of our poesis, our contrived patterns of words and sounds in a speech often far elevated above the mundanity of everyday conversation. What better pursuit of communality can there be? Can one place a price on this and would one want to?

This sharing of poetry has generated a chain of continuity which flows into the acknowledgements I would like to make, but realizing the world of poetry is vast, there are many more than cited, and I hope I am forgiven for those I haven't remembered formally for they are legend and part of my ever present parallel universe.

Peter Wadds Jeffery, OAM
2015

Cynara! the night is thine;
And I am desolate and sick of an old passion,
Yea, hungry for the lips of my desire:
I have been faithful to thee, Cynara! in my fashion.

from 'Non Sum Qualis Eram Bonae Sub Regno Cynarae'
—Ernest Dowson, *The Poems and Prose of Ernest Dowson*

Love Carnal, Romantic and Family

A Poem in Love to My Wife

Outside, the cars drift with erratic stop and start,
No more than corpuscles in a flow of blood.
Even footsteps with no feet die in the air
Senseless as the wind that knocks our door.

This last night, when my lust unannounced
Grew irritant in our prevailing checking words;
Yet announced, that frustrate desire had spent
Itself in the silent set-to of your consent,
As if, breath held from my last dive,
I was forced into breath again.

Then the gentle climb up the ladder,
Where set to, fell to, held to,
Your rungs peeled off in my hand
And I fell down in a white rush upon your down,
Half held, half fled,
We sank into each other's arms and made our bed.

And envoy of such sweet melancholy,
How many times must we essay to fight,
And always fail in flight,
To win excuse from all fighting?

Sunderland, 1970

King's Park

Twin heart beating, sorrow eyes fleeting,
Stars icing the velvet night,
Grass sings waves as dark winds fight,
Tree-lines glowing in motor-noise flowing.

Warm love lining the flesh-love pining
For male rough embrace;
Latent fingers tracing the shade of face,
Tender heart repining, with twin arms entwining.

Soft speech husking, woman scent musking,
Nerve-lined nostrils with fragrant flower,
Hips soft burning, chest muscles yearning,
Eyes deep night etching the final gem-stars shower.

Perth, 25 August 1954
Published Centaur, 25 August 1954

Two Together: Two Apart

To try to reach back in the void,
To remember the way the word forms in the mouth,
Something between the tongue and the teeth
With wind and spittle and gunmetal taste,
As in running through and beyond oneself,
And the dream of the aching and blessed lave of steaming water,
Turned cool as water around ice in blessed relief.

To weep a little at all the lost days
When one might have conjured the great white horse Pegasus,
And straddled across its back with one's thighs
Warmly melding into the great firm barrel of bone and heave
And roaring into the air, all fluttering as Pegasus,
As strong eagle carving the air
Above the domains etched by river and road
And fence and errant wall and powerline and rail
And any line limning the page of the human frontier.

The thought that all this drum belting and yet another poem to
poetry
Must drop beyond invocation into that dark faltering hollow
Of narrative, and so we turn
Liked timid stutterer to the task and the hope.

I remember the hollow of your groin
Cupping up to hold the pudenda,
The erstwhile pubic scrolling and the sense of honeyed oil
In a moment or was it a land of ever running moistness,
And the sweat happy and the breathing musky,

But solidly thrusting in its joyous effort,
And no more than the window away from us,
The Guildford Swan slipped and slid
Dark under the starry night
Holding its own deep dream of unyielding ecstasy.

Elsewhere two others slept in lonely beds
With who knows what dreams of lovers in shady bliss
Marked by our detaching anger and mutual thrust,
And a sheer animal humour brings the grin out in us
Not with the rictus of climax,
But the sheer leap of the young bodies in silvered lust.

The moon slides away as I drown in your eyes and hair and thighs.

c. 1964

Jazz Piano in a Fernleafed Nightclub

Soft slow railyards of sound weeping out the wax on candles,
And the twinkling glass of crystalled keys,
All these, the piano of that doleful musicman,
Drinking out stars of love and blues
From a stained glass and chewed cigarettes.

We sit there, you and I, watching,
Watching the shadowy spider web of hair mist your face,
And the little pine trees of shading creeping my face,
And our words are little sobs of sorry acceptance.

Then you see an errant flicker of the glad times
And you seize my hand and lead me,
Lead me out on the fernleafed floor,
And our tired feet with sad shoes scutter away the sadnesses.

Comes the slow taxi crawl up the canyoned street
And the light spilling doorstep and the steady kiss,
And the door closes and you clamber into your soft bed aching,
And I walk the cigaretted street home
Watching cars spray fresh water over dust drenched heart.

Perth, January 1957

The Day Dies on Troubled Pages

The day dies on troubled pages.
The acropolis burns irritatingly in the mind.
My eyes quarry the lines like the honeysuckers overhead,
But there is no sweetness at the end of probing.

My wife draws on the tripod of my knees.
The flies fat as bees hang desultorily on my moving foot,
Uncaring in the oceanic warmth, bemused by the pleasant odour,
Till the foot kicks its irritation away.

Yet a peace in the contemplation of our yard —
forests of thistles — tongue tipped bayonets,
little bird lost in the redness of flowers,
green grape leaves fighting for space,
dark drenched yellow butterfly,
grass high — creepers contend both on toilet and tree.

The rug we rest on
a haven from the TQ cars outside,
That puncture the silence like pneumatic drills.

Harvey, Western Australia, 23 October 1960

The Physical Fact

The physical fact was that you were there,
And the sun was silver shoals in the river,
And the ferry was buffeting, and office workers were tired,
And a drunk old lady had sung us a song
And told of her children no longer loving, no longer living.

No longer living ……….
I could feel the plush on the seat,
And your sweet soft face smiling:
But no longer loving,
Making the intertwined cathedral of our hands
Unsatisfactory prayer to a sightless god.

I had watched you
Come out to the bus, the cosmopolites
Tumbling about you, and the strained smile
As you saw me, as if you had the duty
Of putting unneeded flowers on an unknown grave,
And I was quiet in the soft snarling of the traffic.

The physical fact was that you were there,
But to me it was as if two strangers sat
Close, half frightened in the darkening hall
Of the evening sun.
Even as the gull struck at the sinking crust,
I knew it could not rise appeased.

We stood in the dark outside your room,
Shared with another; strange female apparatus
And my little clay teddy bear, half chipped
Upon the shelf. My words were tired wings
Fluttering in vain against the curved glass dome
Of your thoughts. My lips were rough,
My hands made violent jungles in your hair,
You wept — but still it was not there!

Muswell Hill, United Kingdom, 1970

A Chinese Rope Trick

for Paula in affection and friendship

Elegant as a flowing dragon in his silk kimono,
At Tara's birthday, the Chinese magician
Called two children to hold taut a golden cord,
Then in illusion tied it as a knot
And with a blade cut through its loop, covered it in red cloth,
And with strange words and a casual flick
Shook it free to reveal
The rope once more without knot in
Its line pure and straight.

A subtle magic, but not so sharp
That adult, I did not see
The palmed piece of rope,
Bent into a knot,
Move from his flowing sleeve
And after the cut return there.

To us then,
Perhaps I was not yet too tired
To believe in magic,
The 'one-more-time' that renders
The everyday — the mundane — illusion
And so in romance,
Then it was, I asked you
To cross the line
To make age and circumstance
Pure lines of flight.

But because you did not see what I saw —
Snap of the fingers it is/was not there —
This poem stands its lines in that place.

And now past that tangle of hope and dubious emotion,
And having said such things
Which I wished were said,
I am bemused by my own folly,
Wondering if we shall leave those lines now unsaid.
Stronger than and longer than any rope,
We move to the straighter lines of friendship and art;
Past your shy smile of embarrassment
That partly flares the eyes
And dances below your flushing cheeks
Along the lip-line hesitant in its speech,
So our awareness with its trace of comedy,
Strengthens a future path lined with good humour.

Still the languor of longing remains.
And as with Marion we know there are lines,
There are lines everywhere.
We are/were a knot of vectors,
The ambulant armatures of our solitary rooms;
Our 'lignes de fuite' taper to disappearance.
And so we sit/sat there,
The sudden chill of near midnight
Dancing along the line of your modest blouse,
Above the simple functional army trousers,
And we watch each other
The cappuccinos, the table and away
To catch other lines.

We see/saw a sardonic Godardian joke,
Where two lovers mimed against the flatness of wall
An extreme passion, a flagrante delictio
In a moving mouing graffiti,
With the elegant entwining of her white stockings,
His dark trousers, starkers.

Near us people eat, as with Marion,
So that the oiled garlic spaghetti unravels
As the fork plies its route from plate to mouth.
Until somewhere between Papa's and Gino's,
In the flashing blue flare of the Maria,
Our Pulcinello with a flagon of abandon —
An old nyoongah comic with his gerber —
Meanders the median.

And in a gentle melancholy
I would that that we had sung each other
Through the long lines of trees,
Beyond the camp, the fires and waterhole,
Into each other's bush — its sweet oblivion.

At once, restless one night,
I dreamed the ocean between the groynes,
Its thin line stretching between isles,
Tumbling its waves,
And I stretched for the thin line of phone
Where Griff's birds might be found lightly pecking
And whistling smiles into your ears and eyes.

Remembering Marion one more time —
'From the brow upwards there are lines, knots,
But somehow the perfection of that hemisphere
Is not marred'-
I muse that like the architect in Rome,
The thin hair, the erstwhile line of eyebrows,
The strong lines and folds of my belly
Make their own intense elegance,
And we lure each other
With our lines of white and red ribbons
Past suggestive silhouette
Behind the obscurity of a cream white blind unlit.

And now,
These things said
I would have this poem —

These words —
Whiter than any blank page
In a book unopened
Beyond the reach of all speech,
And marked with no offence.

1991

Sonya's Toys

And these things unfolding:
Exploding sensation for sight and skin.

Sensate, but as yet not given proper name,
But softness for skin, companion in waterways,
Dear warmth of colour, roughness for teeth,
Jangling ricochet of plastic on tensile string,
Their squeaking startle evidences a patterning world.
The platypus solid ramrod of beak and fur,
The corn rattle, thanksgiving for deep harvest,
Mother Duck and family, a waddling saga through infant time,
Red Reynard, duckling bright eyes and tickling tail,
All adult chosen to illuminate reality,
To create pleasant fantasies.

But now,
You lie in your peace
Of water coolness, rocking pram, roll on towel
And flight through air.
Your toys stand silent for the fairy wand of age.

Nedlands, Western Australia, c. 1962

That Joy Should Have a Form

That joy should have a form;
That a spirit be as substantial as your little finger
That your smile should abstract joy
O little one.
Joy is compound.

Nedlands, Western Australia, c. 1962

Magpies

for Clifton Pugh

Cultivated in the peace of city parks,
Their voracity of probing beak is half myth
On children's lips and in wild wide eyes.
Yet malignity turns to domesticity —
Scalped hair is the wall of their nest.

Out here on the hill's quiet side,
Where mystery is revealed in every cool shade
Their true nature comes, and half cousin to the crow,
They drive the dog from his meat,
And probe down the long sinews of steak,
Drawing tendons as fine as any surgeon's knife.

They are, in evil,
Unhurried and as noncommittal
As the coffin black of their wings;
Their eyes black, yet audacious,
Their violence custom and dulled by long use.

As long as dying eyes watch, and stop watching,
They will hold ambush, these snipers of the flesh,
Till the knee crooks, the flank subsides
And phobic eyes glaze into royal jellies.

From them, then, there is no need
For ants and the mute complicity of the final soil,
While the flesh drawn in long streamers
Buffets the air,
In the lone labyrinth of their intestinal walls.

Darlington, Western Australia, c. 1965

Breughel Near Penshaw

Toiling the hill,
A child on my back,
Sundered from Sunderland we walked the neglected track,
In search of the stolen sun,
And slipping down the coils of the Lampton Worm,
We fall stumble across the potato shucker's tracks
Where schoolchildren gouge out hidden spuds
Oblivious to us in their own pursuit.

We, in search of selves like plucking blackberries,
Three generations held out in a line of walking
Under the wires of girders
Yet watching the scouring of that field -
Those children rough as sacks
Natural they in search of cash or spuds,
Natural we in search of sun.

As ordnance maps etch the slightest ruction of the earth's throat,
I outline eulogies for we four in our contained worlds
As pristine and lucent as a Bosch sphere in Eden garden
And end up leapfrogging those worlds over each other
As boisterous and uncouth as Breughel's schoolboys.

Sunderland, 1970

We Live in a World of Music
for the Quath Family

We live in a room of music.
The little girl is learning her future
By drawing endless zeroes,
Like falling leaves on the page,
And as her pencil moves
She hums and sings
Like a fledgling breaking into thin song.

We live in a house of music,
Where the youth of the internet,
The mobiles, the endlessly moving bikes
Sing their dreams in the karaoke
Of the new world, their electronic voices
Thundering to the nearby mountains,
Or sighing like the wind of the nearby sea.

We live in the streets of music,
Where I hold a girl on her bike
And her hair streaming,
And I hear her voice
Hungering for your touch
On a long lonely night,
As I hunger for the touch of Vietnam,
As we go roaring and streaking through the streets.

We live in the folk clubs of music,
Where a blind musician sees
Through his fingering music
Visions of Vietnam brighter than any noon sun.

Around him the common people,
Join and joy in happy song,
Making and tracing the history
Of heroes, of love, of struggle, of creation,
Against the beauty of Vietnam's ever changing seasons.

We live in the five point stars of music,
For our heaven and earth is here and now
From our daily food of fish, rice, flesh,
Fruit — all in rainbow of taste,
To the hills of Sapa, the isles of Halong,
The Delta and the sea of Phuoc Hai
For wherever we are, we are the song of Vietnam.
We live forever in the world of music.

Phuoc Hai, Vietnam, 10 January 2004

Snowman

Ice white the day.
Snow holds the blue – metal in frozen mulch,
Where normally, it would be endlessly shifting,
Under moving, scuffling shoes,
And huge cars
Spinning their half curve,
Under huge revving wheels.

The boy talks of snowmen,
Phantoms from storybooks,
And his father shudders
At the memory of endlessly balled snow,
Piling upwards past feet,
Knees, buttocks, belly, breasts, head, ears,
And coal-black eyes,
To flesh out such frozen dreams.

The wisp of a child's energy,
Quickfire along the frozen rim of age,
Brings an echo of joy
To this house of adults,
And suddenly the father
Has caught his son's tiny hands
And blown warmth into them,
And then, in a couple, they have
Danced around the snowman
And collided into him,
And in a dervish whirl,
Bring about his collapse
And theirs.

They rise,
And walk back into assured warmth,
While the wind
Drifts across the silent yard,
Over the last lumps,
And the coal black eyes
Stare up at the snow of drifting clouds.

Mount Lawley, January 1996

Half in Love with Easeful Death and Self-Regard

Five I Spent

Five I spent in an old winery,
And as I drank, I tasted His strong brown body,
And all night long I lay sickerly.

Five I spent in a house of harlotry,
And as I felt, I stabbed His nailed agony,
And all day long sores covered me.

Five I spent for a seat at a crucifixion,
And as I watched, His eyes seared flames through me,
And all night long I tossed in misery.

Five I spent on musicmen's revelry,
And as I heard, His voice shattered thunders in me,
And all day long noise pierced me.

Five I spent on Arab perfumery,
And as I smelt, the myrrh of His shroud overcame me,
And all night long my nostrils flickered nervously.

The other five I spent on waxen candles for Thee,
And as they burnt, I prayed sorrowfully,
And all day night long I hung twisted about a Judas tree.

Perenjori, March 1957

Canary on the Edge of Dying

In the half dusk of my homeward going,
I saw a sudden gold orb dancing in lavender,
That was slowly melding this way and that,
Into the fluttering of a canary.
I halted, self-arrested in a near endless gaze
Until I was driven to desire it,
Sweetly palpitating in my enclosing hand.

I moved forward — thus — to invite it,
Almost too sudden, so stepped abruptly back
Into a wary stillness, lest I frightened it
Away into the air, losing it
In the sudden as I had first found it.

I hovered as it hovered
In its domestic desire,
Wishing for earlier human attention
And its caged return to seed and water.
But then I felt in thought —
"Let it be — for it is free!"
And so I walked past it
To walk on to the warmth and light of home.

Later, alone, I thought of the ever-enclosing darkness,
And what might be of the length or briefness
Of the canary's flight,
Its soft golden orb dimming
Into the darkness, the blank blackness of night.

Mt Lawley, 29 December 2012
Published in Regime, 2014

London Cemetery

I see tears in the dew.

Amongst the graves, the golden summers of daffodils,
And in the mausoleum, pigeons as fat as hens
Mourning their voices.

The sparse elegance of the scientific grave,
The information notated in crisp dates,
The experiment of life concluded,
The electric bolt of Faraday forever absorbed in his moist cell.

Along the wall, above the bickering weeds,
The plaque of Marvell once dwelling here,
A Latin Secretary of State, wit, satirist,
But he had not world enough and time.

Landseer, a stag's head small as medals,
The printing in metal on polished stone,
The rain melting the strength into the obscurity of pavements,
And the melodrama of tangled weed and hauntling vault.

But the great matter not.
There are sagas enough in this chaos of stone,
Without the ornament of proud names.
Each draped urn, each wooden cross, each vain heart
Marks out the fear and glory of two hundred years.

I am alone with the sparrows,
The long amphitheatre of vaults,
And my thoughts.

I see tears in the dew.

Tufnell Park, 1958
Published Westerly 1958; ABC Women's Session, 8 January 1960; and
The Bulletin 1960.

On a Visit to St Joseph's

The automatic signature of the cross,
The holy water salt on the fingers,
The familiar, mysterious dark of the vault,
The twisted simplicity of Christ,
And finally that splendour of gold and robe and candle.
I was no stranger.

Yet scantling fear ran round the masonry of my heart,
Hemming my humility in, holding the confusion down,
So that I could not pray,
To make proud converse of selected word and phrase
To my Lord.

The proud blasphemies had no wings,
My faith was still a war in the blood,
And yet,
As I left, I felt a certain tolerance,
As of a bear watching its cubs at play.

Harvey, Western Australia, c. 1960

The Outsider

He is of life;
Eats the bread we eat, frequents the stool,
Slops the spaghetti strands,
Complains the weakness of watery beer,
Mounts the wire caged harlot in tattered bed.

Yet he is not with us;
For he views his misery in the pool of the drunkard's vomit,
Cries at the Bible text printed in a fornicating tram,
And swears at the cold wind nuzzling his jute bare coat.

Rather is his pillow stars,
His thoughts cypressed flames,
his words broken glass.
And he scuffs the asphalt as a hermit would desert sand.

Endlessly, he walks the junk-yard street of life.

Perth Public Library, 1956

For Those Dying

For those dying, walls flare into sheets,
Or ooze white cream into their nostrils,
Sculpting the air that husks,
Or dribbles golden
Down the sides of their mouths —
Jewels as vital as the strobe lamps on ambulance
And as permanent as the dampness
Of cleaner swept streets.

But for us living, the pheasant dulls on the butcher's stand,
Lemons crinkle golden into mouldering brown,
Rivers run gutters of litter, clouds suppurate smog,
Shining limousines shatter into rust,
And the entire world is a sempiternal
Cataract in our eyes.

c. 1957

Soft Steps

Death calls its own ritual.
Mystery is not telegraphed along the wall,
The stations are rather the beds.

Here there is the silence of soft steps,
The little sacramental tablets to ease the world sorrow.
The silent drawing of gloves on hands,
The steady surge of bubbles in oxygen,
The ikon of fluttering lives aspiring to
The angelic needlepoint of release.

c. 1955

Fixed Between Camden Lock
and London Zoo

I sat down in a boat on Regent Canal and fixed.

Pumped along the arteries of London,
I saw the stroboscope of chill and sun,
And felt the bars of the tiger behind the rippling cage.
Green branches snaked along the trunks
Of trees giraffing their leaves over leaves,
Envying the smooth girders of air
That held down birds under heavens of wire.
Saw the split plane fused by dynamite
And iron Doric under-bridges to hold
In the darkness of imagination,
That had slid in fog through the tunnels,
Where no one had confidence to echo,
And had run up to the walls of wooden indifference,
Cooling towers dripping silence.

c. 1970

The Lecturer Discusses 'Lady Chatterley'

Half voyeur, half exposeur,
He voyaged through exposition,
Legs crossed, but trousers hitched,
Hairy calves above his socks,
And from his thin-lipped mouth
Came unsurprisingly
Sensually overblown shocks.
His audience captive as a harem,
Every girl was cynically consigned
To the bed of literary imagine,
Where he lay reclined
In a fairground of stressed innuendo,
And upright he was ringmaster
With all the girls over-bend-o.
He hoop-laed joyously
Through all their disgusts,
Till they scurried thankfully into the recess sun,
And he retreated gown flying
Up the stairs, his soul crying
To be understood
At his most perverse good.

Sunderland, 1971

Houseboat, Yunderup

All lit up and no place to go!

Now in the time of the Passion,
The river is aflare with waste.
Water creams forever across the estuary flats
And like great stranded porpoises,
Fat beche-de-mers lie on houseboat decks,
Bikini brown prows on flamewhite cabin covers,
And like tired drovers' horses,
Forever chained to the bar rails,
The houseboat lumbers slobbering up and down.
While its $100 a week crew
Booze their way through the Yunderup store,
From red to green to purple,
And bombard each other with chocolate shells,
Or sleep till the amber tide swirls,
Past Easter Sunday into Monday.
Christ's carnival is barbecued flesh.

Only the racing gulls in April's wind
Swirl four tear wounds across the river,
The ibis monstrances against drowned gum,
And baleful silver slashes dark cloud
To myself, silent cynic, a memory
Bloodier than the reddest veined egg.

Guildford, Easter Monday, 1974

To Retreat into Poetry for the Hour

To retreat into poetry for the hour,
To suspend anxiety,
To return to unremarked breath
And a fixed gaze on the three lines
Of beach, sea and sky,
Like a geometer's dream
Of brilliant parallels and marked domains.

Outside the rubbish truck clangs
Its way down the street, house by house,
And bustles the bins
Into a return of emptiness,
And an assertion of new order
For the fresh detritus and residue
Of busy workaday days,
And in a sense, he wishes not to believe
In this diurnal round,
Well past Wordsworth's notions of sky and rock,
And sleeping transforming form,
Feminine, masculine or impartial neuter.

The words assemble and even clutter cluster
On the page to mark the hour,
With the breathing of words —
The endless ladder of black on white,
That creates blocks of story and concepts.

But the story will not come so easily
Nor has it ever.

But might it just,
And then, what story could
Match such a withheld promise that leads
Past orgasm and epiphany.

All things lead to a supine dribble.

And yet, still, in the garden
The cat stalks,
The mulberries are black jewels of juice,
And crushed in the hand ,
They leave the indelible stain
Of the active fingers —
Action supersedes concept and brings it into being.

And the halfhour dreams its way,
Silent, with no readers,
No servitors of sense and praise,
The fan in the computer
Drones and his lidded eyes
Are shut in a swound of stupor
Of empty moment.

So where will he go?
Twisting and turning in the moments,
Endlessly flowing away
Irresistibly to the end.

Is he calm?
Not really.

Mount Lawley, Thursday 11 November 2000

Newcastle Street Infants

Looked at again
In the welter of changed buildings,
One wonders what one is seeking,
What infant whisper spawns mature myth.

From our corner, where our memories dig
What was a line of pavilions
With huge openings and blinds
 That flared or blocked out sun,
That zephyred or drummed out the scattering rain.

This corner too looks across a levelling field
With the pavilions all vanished,
But still bound by a long line of trees
Saying what?

The infant voices move through shrillness,
Chirp, chant, criss-crossing choir to brooding babble,
Through Infants to Third Standard
From 'Bubs' to blazered High School.

And still we stand here,
The mystery of rising sap
Thrusting out the aging trees.

Older than any short and unique history
From our single stand,
We make a small memory burgeon
Past transformed rooms

Into that long line of trees,
Rising and falling with the rhythm of years.

2005

Of the Making of Books and Poetry there is No End

Elegy for the Craft of Words

And when he realised, at the loss of a head,
That the milliards of men and years were empty with justification,
Tolstoy forsook the craft of words
To wear a peasant smock and hammer his shoes,
To crumble his tearful pride in a wayside station.

Was a time
When the prince of words was prince of men,
Holding out the gaunt winter wolf with his fiery circle,
And summering swallows lilted
From his chapped lips.

But these debts of disregard had cruel reckoning,
When Autolycus with his basket of ballads
And Falstaff, barrel of words,
Both lost their power in Involvement.
The swallows of song and speech lay smothered in their nests.

Knowing this, patrons bought their lost innocence.
Poets were protected fools,
Masque makers for melancholy moments,
And their sunshone walks were in walled gardens,
While the blast of outside war scoured the plains.

But princes fell and market places rose.
Words were weighed in slabs like cake.
Bad drove out good and standards conformed all in mediocrity.
Still, some starving troubadours babbled to the walls
Of caged swallows and tumbled cities of gold.

Words became docile dogs performing for the State circus,
Their tamers ridiculous in cockroach coats,
And students scattered dandruff from their festering skulls,
While poets burnt in flames of stars
In the darkness of this inhuman space.

The age is ashamed of assonance and alliteration
And fugitive thoughts are packed in sterile rhyme.
Each magic maker is imprisoned, tried and executed
In pedant notes translating all to current orthodoxy.
Words are emolument, distraction, and castrate sexuality.

Enough of bitterness, enough of tears,
Weeping is for a thing of worth that's lost —
There is no loss of glory, no travesty of magic
When metal swallows fly to a neon sun,
Behind windows that neither contract nor expand.

Still outside in Winter's fire
Harp strings slack under ragged cloak,
Poets stumble, speared by lightning,
Wild eyes steaming, raven's hair screaming,
And batter at unyielding doors.

Hollywood, Western Australia, c. 1964

Fireworks

There is a soft beauty in verse;
The irritation of effort is lustred pearl.

O God, Who steeps the final germ
In whirling womb and dark gestation,
Watch the firelight trail of luminous verse,
Acid bright its mouthing depradation —
Filigree of leaves, and tattered pennant
Of rampant weed and upright stem.
Until in sunflamed convolution,
It leaves its poetic carapace —
A final, shuffled coil.

O watch the leaf,
O watch the stem.
Poets die in dwindling orbit,
And the vibrant earth
Trembling in new spring
Scatters long ribbons of fire on the baptized earth.
Poems again spark and carol the dew.

O God, the earth is pyrotechnic,
Firework poets flare and spurt,
And your delight is their joying death.

But, O,
The shattered stumps,
The crumpled fountains,
The silent bombs,
Fizzle their pain in unrequited night.

1970

Poets Have Their Heroes

Watching the puppetry of the established ones,
Evtushenko,
Blonde stilyaga with a Brando cut,
Brooded in the cold square,
Till, hoisted from his anonymity,
By the bobbysoxers of his brusque words,
He blew hot on their consumptive hearts,
And behind, the committee of chagrin and buried words
Composes anger into waxen smiles.

O yes, you children of the mass mind,
Juggernauting in cars, drenched in video,
We have our heroes, and like you,
They are not dead.

Dylan,
Wild thunderer of broadcast words —
A crushed Welsh rose,
The grimy, tattering tottering ash,
Belly squashed hair and eyes
Bulbous as berries with the good words —
His milkwood chilling
In the fey scamper of babbling elves,
And parsons draper mad in the breast soft snow.

Hopkins,
Baffle bound in his bone house,
While gale high,
The darksome sweep of windhover wings

Holds air and fields, fettle, fall,
All for the plots and gears
Of his reintight words.

Lorca,
Word mad under negro guitars
And bosoming moon uddersacked over the rosy
Trellis of his star scattered mind.
His cadenza of death — Falangist guns.
Your gypsy heart,
Dark and slumbrous as blood thick words,
Flutters dovelike in all our eyes.

Poets have their heroes,
Teller of tales taller than life,
Brave as any butting billy boy in football flame,
Crooner more bop than the take and break of a Brubeck Bach,
Huskier, duskier, as thigh mad as skipping wenches
Broad buttocked, blousy breasted, Monroe misted,
Corn blue — oh the biggest milkshake of all this world.

1970

Intense

Intense.
As the mayfly above a trout
The trout beneath the mayfly.

Poem is a journey
Hawk trailing wind from the fence.
Paint this book. Paint this scene

Detail
Gone mad and fey,
Take the bramble, take the weed,
Take the marked stone,
Burn, beck, dene, dyke, wick,
Beneath the sea the coral stirs
Blood poured onto stone
Into earth,
Druids and fox and wandering gone mad,
Romance floods the mind,
As the gusty gutsy wind
Flames across the grass.

1971

They Have Come, John, For Your Soul

They have come, John, for your soul.
Old Nick and Beezlebub, and a goat with straggly hair.

Ye canna run to the old grandpa clock,
And that poker'll do you little good,
And John, it's no use going in there.
Ye look like a little beetle
Running from a taper.
If you weren't in death John
We could both laugh together.

Ye scream a little now me boy?
Remember Hades is hot and fear.
Ye cry for mercy, lad,
Ye who cut a heathen's whimpering head,
Laughing all the while.

'tis no use acrying, accursing, or abegging,
it's only wild wind in your throat.
Old Nick's got blinden eyes,
Beezlebub's deaf in both ears
And the other's just a goat.

Goodbye John, I'll drink your health,
In wine as black as bats,
And when the witches run in the molten sky
I'll tell my childer about old John,
Nick, Beezlebub and a straggly old goat.

c. 1953

Paris Town is a Long Way Away

Oh the night was dark when we shipped her,
Shipped her down the stream.
The shore was blackened hulks,
And the stars a sky of gulls.

Ned was drunk on cider,
On cider was he drunk,
And the little cabin boy wept
His salting tears into the foaming prow.

My jumper was thick around my neck,
My neck was warm with wool,
And I laughed at the fallen snow
Blossoming of almonds in the devilish blue.

I've sailed in Chinee towns,
In Chinee towns I've drowned,
Beneath a wave of flowing silk
And in a sea of sweetened smoke

In a far off Indy temple,
Temple with turrets of melting gold,
I've heard the sounding gong
Make thunders in my head.

Yet in all my roving days,
And in my days I've roved!
I never sailed on sorrow struck ship
As Christ-thorned as this.

The captain took his bride to sea,
And she died of leprosy,
The cook cooked octopus,
 And died with tentacles around his neck.

A storm took us asunder,
Broke our timbers with thunder,
Surfed me ashore,
With ten lost teeth and a broken Jaw.

c. 1955

The Ganges Delta

'Oh you! You speak like the Ganges delta!'

Diffusing, muddying and finally annoying
I speculate in a gush of words,
Confident in my tentativeness.

> 'Be precise!
> The object is definitely one inch long.
> Truth should not balance on analogy
> But on the pure needlepoint of precision.
> To measure is to understand!'

Your flea of truth bites
And I itch all over.
More precise by far
Than that Irish bard's
'Rose, rose! Rose of all our days.'
In Greenwich, the yard
Was yard of all yards.
And now, the Paris meter
Thrust by world convention
Measures every single thing —
Careful, precise, metriculous!

Yet in that imperial metre
Atoms older than Napoleon
Mill around, avoiding each other
Trying to approximate the truth
Of the idea that is precision itself.

WAIT, Bentley, 1973

Myth as Mist and Meaning

Hemispheres apart, as in the slant of a dying sunset,
Misty meaning dances across to, in and around opposing myths.

I go looting lives for narrative,
The search for a myth in one day, in one city,
To recount in our evening's salon and conversatz.
Did a worm lie along the Dart, longer than Lambton,
And did it mean the same as the antipodean Rainbow Serpent?

So that here in Devon, in a dusky, gusty shade
I echo the long strand of Broome and chance that resonance,
Tinny, scrawny as the croak of mopoke,
Against a European sussurus that caresses
The polished flanks of the endlessly repeated David.
More like Hughes trying to lime down Britain to a stick or branch
With his ungainly, but sharp beaked and flailing, squawking Crow.

Their companionate figures held mutually to their merging shadow —
He, the Western tracer and placer of myths walks with him
The keeper of symbols and sacred sites,
Every landmark mnemonic and told in a diurnal circular trek,
Each story owned by a tribal member and sustaining them,
Together, through endless retellings
Of an agreed morality that defies collapse and event.

The story's simple enough!
A young woman leaves her old husband's stale and diddling embrace
To dance limber and ecstatic with the athletic lover,
Singing her from the trees.
Until in the still glaze of high noon —

Their elopement slopes long shadows
Ever further and further from his futile limbs
And all forms to a tapestry of desultory pursuit.

Breathlessly chasing, provocatively pacing,
The pursuer and the pursueds mark out the mythic distance,
Until in an avenging thunderbolt, that shafts in coeval ricochet,
Moving littoral apart, the spear of righteous hate
Blasts her lover aside,
And homes phallically to wrench her legs apart —
Flagrante made flagrant —
Leaving her shattered remains as twin rocks,
Definite and solitary as the enactment of a final curse,
Where adultery and retribution are etched in landscape,
Like some satirist's classical dictum —
A landmark of a morality
That endures far beyond a single day's mere telling.
Myth and neuroses have a common core —
The desperate search for a God and His attributes.

The wise aboriginal tries
To hold down his culture by such a telling,
To make solid that mere integument that marks the sexes
Into a contract of permanent rigidity,
Given to the semiotician who is already adulterous
Out of wife and capable of any fluctuation in sexual exchange,
Just like his own culture's whitest knight
Sullied all for, and by a queen's love,
And in that moment, his lance and head were forever
Sloped to the ground in shame,
And could not uplift, no matter how bright the sun
Calling to battle for his king.

My retelling this becomes
Post-structuralist myth,
Deracine,
A smooth mirror shattering the shield for Medusa.

Totnes/Devon, England, 10 February 1995

An Imaginary Poet and Location

for Kenneth Seaforth Mackenzie

I am striding through your poetry
As you strode through the river flats,
The whitened chapel behind you,
As English and as removed,
As the gumnuts and scree of windblown trees
Around us both
Is Australian and intense.

I hope to be blinded by your epiphany,
And so see the ant as mighty emblem,
The lemons on neglected trees as orbs of gold,
So that I will know this place
Where you and I once lived
As source of ever revealing wonder
The recurring phoenix pyre
Of that weird Rosella Poetry
Slicing the air left and sliding right
Winging straight to glory.

All I hear is the scrunch of my shoes,
Feel the burrs work into my snagging socks,
The impatient wiping of congealing sweat
And know I have missed you
And your secret.

It is only in the retreat
Of the daunted quest
That I summon up cool shadows
Of resignation and melancholy
And pacing slowly and tiredly

Through the darkening
Suddenly I am in that other place
Of pure plunging ecstasy
In the stream of the drowned orchard
Where you fatally saw
The trailing resolve of final poetry
That hymns object as verse
And verse as object.

Mt Lawley, 24 September 1996

A Song for Sorensen

I know you, man
Dark, despite your chosen word,
gracious phrase, and myth making.
I know you!
I paused over my work of words
To hear and see your words
And even felt the ship go to Queensland
The northern, not the southern route,
And I know you
In your last black fight
As you subsided.

A songmaker lives in his audience,
And though they tell of you
As a mere ad hustler
That was not the man.
For you was the joy
Of the remembered word,

But new blood, new needs,
The academic has no time for you today,
The common man has forgotten you,
And you are alone
In the wind of your voice.
I know you
And your need,
That is why I write a song for you.

2006

The Dimming Light
for Noelann Gandon

With her sharp alert eyes and page-boy or even monkish cut,
And that abrupt stab of cigarette, held so languidly the moment before.
She could so easily have been the pantomime boy,
And flattened down for Peter Pan,
Or would it be Puck?

For what need had she of that?
For with her extended arm and flick of palm,
She had a total and directorial will
That could conjure up —
As you like it —
Cleopatras, Joans, Lady Bracknells, Lysistratas, Ophelias
Or what you will to please us all.

Yet her own body in its stance
Had a sense of pure theatre
So that some of us would rather watch her
Behind the scenes or in the director's seat,
Than anyone she drew across the stage.

Brown as a berry, and hard as a nut,
She was sharp bramble and delicate rose
And rich fruit and everywhere.

In mock disbelief and suspended optimism,
She regarded the world with her skeptic's eye
Forever skipping, dancing, darting.

But with her gentle deprecation yet generous regard,
She hardened us for disappointments that might come,
Yet softened us in humour with each and every success,

Trimming our ambition to a proper sense of itself,
Allowing us to be light with a most serious purpose.

Sweating in the Murdoch arena —
Her new theatre open to the pines, the stars, the skies —
I remember her like an Egyptian taskmaster
Levying the volunteer student slaves
As she called out this small task and that —
Yet no sooner said than done herself!

For she refused to wait
For what might rightly come,
And once, impatient amongst loving friends,
Even brought on
The Midnight of the New Year
Hours before
With her own delighting and imperious rush.

As demanding teacher, she ran the canon of drama
And lashed any student who neglected a period —
Greek, Roman, Shakespearean, Restoration —
Determined to show that each age had its own logic of theatre,
And that the absence of this knowledge was vulgar and boorish.

In theatre she disdained flatulent talk
Of what might be, should be, could be
For she always knew what would be!

Her intellect was in her action!
Shrewd moves of thought were strokes of paint on the flat,
The tuck of the costume, the flash of the head, the pointed toe,
And the relentless ever rehearsing of the repeated but ever varied lines —
And she even hafted the head onto the spearman's staff.

And my next to last memory
Was of us on a sandy beach,
Climbing a twisting erstwhile hilly path,
To search for her Bremer Bay house nearby or hereabouts,
To find her at the head of her haven,

Staring down as if our visit was as regular and commonplace
As if from the daily milkman,
Rather than a three year absence and friendship's drought.

And by her a small dog ran,
But mistily I saw a sheepdog, well out of his clime,
And as medieval as Chaucer,
Big as a moving haystack, grinning foolishly,
Bumping against her, tangling its rope and trying to tumble her feet,
And by her side a gruff but loving man,
Who delightfully drowned me with gin,
As we gazed down some passing sunset as colonial and imperial as India —
'Hot curry and pukka, sahib' and 'What say you, sir?'
and then in the ever present now,
she moved us past the flying angel in the garden
and into her house for a slice of cake and a cup of tea.

So many friends, so many Noelanns,
So many gifts, so many thanks,
Each of us has a poem for her,
An essay of love in its truest sense,
And she will justly mark them all,
But secretly be pleased
That her work is a footnote for all our lives.

In Rome they said that when she went
A breath had gone from the world
Making it the lesser for it.

Or is she that sprite of breeze that moves across Bremer Bay —
That Southern doctor of our late afternoon,
With its rush of memory and nostalgic love —
As in pale imitation,
We watch the sunset from her seat,
With our paperback, our cigarette, and our cold glass of wine?

An Old Friend, Mt Lawley, 2000

Cable Television—The Sinking of *The Titanic*

No worries the hackwriter said,
TV plots are simple,
They're only combinations.
Take the unlikelies,
A drunken bellboy who once was a monk
With a cop who dresses in his wife's clothes
And a lady gardener with a vegetable child
All stuck in a lift,
With the building closed down for a four days' holiday,
Then fetid air, no food, no water,
And a thousand dollar script.

Guildford, 8 June 1973

A Camel in Japan

If man meets woman they make love;
If A and B then surely C!
But if A is a priest, a butcher, a soldier, a clerk
And B is a nurse, a teacher, a soubrette, a nun,
Then priests meet nurses and forgive syphilis,
      Butchers meet teachers and short change,
      Soldiers meet soubrettes and chant rape,
      Clerks meet nuns and order habits.
So men take camels to snowy Japan,
Where they chew cuds and contemplate slopes
Of Fuji, then turn to concrete bars
And spit.
One might as well take a Camel to snowy Japan,
And light it and watch it slowly smoke and burn.

Guildford, 8 June 1973

In Friendship is All

Saintly Sinner

for Bill Grono

What to say, when we know each other too well,
Yours to kiss and tell, mine to see and say
So let us emblazon Grono as legend,
Along with the irate landlord, creditor, bastard
Hammering your door,
Shouting 'Grono, Grono, I know you're there. Grono!'

College days with your mentorship
Parallel to those pedagogues Chiron and Centaur,
Strength to stand against censorship,
Showing the hypocrisy of whispered statement,
And the honest strength of literary declaration.

Ingenious like incipient Murdochs,
With our instant roneos of the inter-colleges carvnival,
Long before internet.

Literature aside, I see you
Somewhere in the haze near Haig and Zanthus
Walking towards us,
Not long after the squared paper ran out
And the coloured pencils blunted or broke,
Across that desert Nullarbor.
Thin you were as a sapling, wiry as mulga,
Like Lawson in a 'BULLETIN' caricature.

From ocean to ocean we trekked
Hiding behind railcarts, bent double,
Until a flat-top revealed us to the friendly guard.

He sung in the season against the heat,
'A merry syphilis and a happy gonorrhea!'
Dousing that vulgarity with romance and nostalgia,
With sadness and melancholy, about his concubine,
His Madam Butterfly with delicate feet and shiny kimono,
In a garden world with him like a samurai lord,
Before he had to return to sterile Australia.
As we sat, our legs trailing at the back of the box car,
The rails endlessly unravelling before our feet.

A trek so full of image,
Sudden sharp stabs of returned memory,
The paradox of the halt at a deserted station
Half formed as a solitary pub
Where we enter the door that barrels its passage
To the back door and shows the empty void of endless desert.
We poured our drinks and left a pound note for the phantom barman.
And journeyed into the paradox of Snowtown,
with its century of blistering heat,
and avoided the brutal darg of unloading Gambier stone,
for payment for our lift, by jumping the train
into suburban Adelaide, where we avoided capture
by the kindly civic queer,
and travelled on.

Up on the Cross, lost in the 'Arabian'
With the murals of the witch-woman Rosaline,
Outstripping Lindsay's etchings in a perverse orgy
Of half-men/half-women, flames and starry night
That inflamed my onanistic senses,
But you, moved on into your own romance,
Were lost for days in semitic sophistication,
No less dynamite than the barge
I strode as it sailed Nobel through the Heads.

In later life, you stand generous in shouted drinks
And slump with a last dying bid
Of your Christmas pay in the Calcutta Stakes
And with your 'tin' you win

And buy an expensive black coat for Europe,
Like Mudie's man who wore an overcoat
In Marble Bar.

Raconteur and confidante of Governor's sons,
Curator of galleries, Rhode scholars,
Learning diction from Snodgrass in respectful modesty,
Despite your 'Silver Swan' award.

One last tale, whether these legends are true or false,
Where you rise from a circle of poets
At the Ocean Beach, and are seen, or are thought to swim,
Out into the ever widening ocean's reach.
Lost at midnight, restored in the Nedland's dawn,
Long may we say,
'Grono, we know you are there!'

Mt Lawley, 2000

The Sixteenth Chair

for John

Loading
The sixteenth chair,
He felt all reason snap
Along the vertebrae of his unwilling patience,
And the convulsive twist of snaking anarchy
Allowed him to balance,
Pivot, and pirouette the chair —
Suiciding Nijinsky in fragile certainty —
On the edge of the backboard
And let it fall
To the uncomprehending road,
That led him to his new home.

Signally marked
By such libation,
A sixteenth splintered chair, significant as the dregs
From a tun of wine,
He moved from real anger to petulance
And almost joy
As he shifted into the seat of the van.
And running through the gears
Of his emotion,
Made that final trip
From today into tomorrow
With nearly all the furniture of his past
Intact.

c. 1970

J P Molony

There are above this earth such stars,
Holding fire in the ice of cloud.

More bright than childhood's eyes
Lost in the hungry groping of bushfires,
You fly in metal flame of tracer.

Your thoughts are wrapped in an old bush school
Or the jungles of Queensland.

But which do you prefer, bushfire, propeller fire, stars?
You race from school at the planes overhead

You are chocked and cocooned in your family
But the tales in the bars
Still ignite the tortuous flare-path between life and death

c. 1957

A December Day in Mary-Land, U.S. of A
for John Daniel

Bugger Southern Comfort!
We'll drink Jack Daniel.

It's my mate John Daniel.
And us with Old Grouse whiskee
And slices of Maryland ham
On ryebread, yeah real eye
And old port cee-gar-illos.
And fizzing like mad
Can-a-da- dry.
While the winter sky
Pops stars all over
The twice frozen ice
Curved and harder
Than blue plas-tic
And the night drifting by
With e.e.cummings, eeeh!
North Country like
On a Library of Congress record
And Jesse Winchester
Working his way across in song
From his Yankee Lady
To Cal-ee-forn-ay.
Us two foreigners
Revelling in the 'Good Life'
To pit face Ph.- Deed
Minnie-apple-is
Or the sunburnt CAE
Of Western Au-strail-yay!

Yah!   Yeah!   Bugger South'n Comfort
We'll drink John Daniel.

Leederville

A Lino of Passing Time and People
Last Work Number 28 (Mural)

Crisp and fresh from the factory we roll out the lino canvas
On the floor of our own new gallery,
And see the squares moving to take up the circle
That makes all colours — red, blue, and invisible yellow —
That in its merging throws up green and lighter orange,
And with the ever present non-colours of black and white,
Make up the light and dark of wisping grey.

Seven of us then take up this surface with the endless pattering
Of our shoes, boots, thongs, sandals and wheelchair tyres —
Linley, Craig, Emma, Graham, Michael, Harry and Clayton —
Skidding and skittering across the shiny smooth surface,
Here, there and everywhere from corner to corner of our canvas
world
To make our mural from all our tracks and paint and personal signs.

Is it hard or easy to see all of us here in this mural?
Linley's subtle dollops in a line like the singing birds
On the branches of a tree,
Craig's strong surge of central black and the softening mist of an
Upper corner,
And Clayton's strong squares and patterned treads,
Helping to hold in the marks and presence of
Emma watching Tony and Graham watching Emma and Tony,
And Harry quiet in his many years watching them like a film.

Murals often make defensive walls,
But by lying flat on the floor of all our studio sessions,
Then hauled up, our mutual mural lino lines the exhibition wall,

We leave ourselves open to all those who pass time to watch and walk
The halls of our world of colour
Where we in turn, have passed time and remembered people.

2010

How Seperately Fused Each to Each

How separately fused each to each —
For one, disdain, another words, another groping love,
Launch pad, crisp notes, widow of science, unrecognized hippiedom.
Prodigal drink, declining drag, hill meditation, painter's formula,
Gangster's tapdance, wisecracking radiocast, sunblast.

Brothers and sisters in embourgeoised time,
Waves break beneath the OBH,
Southern Comfort sours but sparkles in the evening sun.
We are all logics of our situation,
Recast to each other's first premise,
Industry pumps sludge through our streams,
But in sleep, flaming light breaks through our lids our dreams.

Here in rueful fondness, I stake out our sharpest lines —
An old lady goes mad in the street,
Monarch butterflies noted in furthest Western drift
Swirl past America.
Eyeball scalds past blazing eyeball.
In the hospital gardens, ageing, she remembers Shasta daisies.
Edge of the Pale soldiers pot peasants
and peasants pot soldiers like pheasants.
Bruno scales that pain in O'Connor's span.
Suburban birds stalk night above the embered barbecue.
And in the East, the wild woman raves golden up unending stairs.

2004

Brief Friend

Because of the sharp smile
      The tilt of the head
        The twinkling eyes
And the rush and promise of the 'boyo'
I believed there would be shared enthusiasms
And in a way there was
      As the sun died on the veranda
      And the wind dried away into night.

Our speech was stained with pleasant confusions,
Profundities, too far, too loose, to be held.

But when it came to the hard, the physical
The pavement lay there,
The garden remained unweeded.
The house fell slowly apart,
The roof tumbling open with webs,
Untrimmed branches, haphazard blossoms
And like brown nuts
We wrinkled and were gone
In a snap of dust.

2003

Let Us Search for Water

for Michael Selig

'Let us search for water, run its shore,
Give margin to the boundless voids,'
I said that other day,
And you invited me fishing —
Your new found and silent pleasure.
Its memories; chill dawns and warm dusks
With friends and children on holiday
Along the Swan and by the sea,
And I smiled and declined 'til next time.

But, here, now, in Australian Guildford
Friend to our friendship
To search your face
From behind the water
I cast these lines.

In fishing the art is not to expect
The rushing stab and pull of the line
But to watch the listless quiet,
As in Israel, you looked over the Dead Sea
To the hills — mediative trance —
To see where your star of sorrow was shaped
Where your new sun would be born.

First memory, then, is Wales
When you felt out and shaped our pleasure,
For our birthing art and questing hearts,
Your car adding the kindly miles
So that we stood by Dylan's grave

In the cold and whistling air,
Then walked back in the warming rain
To the cheery pub and onto
Hot curry in London —
Our warmth was your adventure.

Always I see you moving
Bright eyes smiling
Amongst fruit and bees,
Bright suns of oranges,
Bright honey in apples,
So that even window cleaning
You stood reflected in sun and blue.

Always, with you, I am driving
Into country, by lakes, by dell,
As in their moment of sorrow
Your children rode
On horse and bike,
To those quiet hills
Around you.

Beneath my hands and unguents
Your shoulders and back relax in luxury.
The sun dances
And freedom beckons —
A little beyond reach
But you beautifully falling there.

No one's thoughts are so truly warm,
To speak a truth
May seem cold, but I know
You valued honesty
As if it were honour.

O lonely boy amongst so many boys,
In that nursery piled with toys,
You seek the kitchen warmth
Of that brusque but kindly cook

And are graced by her care and purpose.
To be the proper man
You try and try and try.
Your sensual chivalry
Moves from concern
With kind surge into passion
And beyond to durable friendship.
The erratic smooths out
Under your gently ironic modesty.

All your life you listened to that silence
Of your own, your child-cry.
No more do you need to catch the mother's eye.
You are to your peaceful self,
You have broken through to that other shore.
By you and with you, now.
Children move and animals stir.

Read at the Funeral of Michael Selig,
South Guildford Cemetery, 2 May 1979

Venturing Through Time and Space

From **Cameos of Sunderland (1970)**

Cameos of Sunderland

Water tower;
city block;
crucifix crane;
desperate train
of smoke trailing
the diesel from the South.
All held in the bridge's
Cameo and its motto,
"Don't despair!"

The Sea

They bought the house
by the sea,
for the sea,
and promptly
forgot it.
Yet above all
their domestic storming,
the North wind blew warning,
so that in bed,
(stones apart in coldness),
the sound of the crashing sea
dashed them together,
into the overrunning foam
of a despairing love.

Bar-room Etiquette

To hold
manners as the final cudgel
of your rudeness
left me
"standing" there
with the hope
that my proffered glass of beer
was as flat as the malice
that made the situation.

Rain Floods the Snow

Fog-horn,
the evening is slow
without you.
Shields to Roker,
the rain drifts in over
your silent absence,
and floods the snow
with a greater grey;
the sea's wet vastness
is not held back
by your measuring bark.

Amateur

As I spoke the intimacy,
he rocked back his head
to see the lemons roll.
And Christ, they were bright, so bright
with the fruit hurtling
down the chute of speech.

And because he had
half an ear
here
     and
        there,
he snapped them all together
into the wallet of his intellect.

But by then
the bloody tumblers had
stopped.

Sunderland, United Kingdom

From *Ostica Antica (1970)*

The City Life

An old cock with a lolling head.
I am too crushed on my foul perch
To clarion down for Ostia,
Morning city of Rome.

Only the gay bantam of delusion
Could strut possibility into such streets
Packed tighter than a pomegranate's seeds
And as tasteless as its chewed pips.

Pallid on this pallet,
With mange in its fur, fleas in its straws,
Even viewing the courtyard raises an itch,
For three goats ram each other,
Kids make a mess on a mound of rubbish
And the chickens foul the last
Dying branch of shade.
Even the bees have flown,
Overswarmed by flies.

I shove past this
And shop at the Thermopolium
Where fine fruit eternally fresh
Hangs pendulous in paint
Above the totting wives
And rotting melons.

I seek retreat in drink
At Augusto's, finding only
North Afric bilge on tap —
The bloody ballast of galleys.

Too hot with such aridity,
In the baths I soak tepidity,
Amongst the chattering queers with withered stumps,
And all touched up.

Or if not dead before dusk,
The theatre with a farce in force;
Where door is changed for door,
Wife for wife, whore for whore,
And the crowd's foolish roar
For my discerning snore.

Or I break free in a midnight run
Along the solitary moonlit shore,
Hoping to kick high spray and sand,
But my sandals scuff fish heads,
And among rocks
My toes stub on the shards of pots.

One Can't Have Gods Enough

The monumental public gods
Accuse the city with their high indifferent stare,
Accept the ostentation of public recompense
Paid by politico and prostitute alike.
Recording, in the finery of their stone drapery,
The Greek sculptor chiselling their stone into filigree on his lungs,
The Afric slave sweating up the hill with their marble blocks,
The histories of cults and guilds and dull official speeches
To mask an inconsequent disturbance in most citizens' lives.

Such gods humble us in the streets,
But do not see the tupping of maids behind the stairs,

The glutting of food and drink,
The cut and thrust of the marital bed.
And as incest is most private and horrendous,
So we make household gods from the squat river mud
Obese, lopsided, smile besmirched into leer,
Eccentric and unique as us;
No, we cannot have gods enough.

The Venus aphrodisiac, throbbing out your sex,
Belly and pudenda distended;
As the serpents twine your legs, make my loving good tonight.
The Mithras bull bellowing against the wall;
Save me from killing him and I'll bathe you in blood.
The Atlas straining against the world;
A bathe of suppliant oil if the rheumatism goes.
Let the moneybags thump like fulsome testes,
For a gold bangle, a shatter of silver flowers.
Turn your eyes as I steal the sweets;
I'll leave you the golden crumbs.

Inconsequence, sequence, essence;
Yes, we cannot have gods enough.

We Are Half Cousin to the Fish

On the Lido, small black Romans eat the fruits of the sea,
Spiked anemone, mussel eye and whorled sea-snail.
Still dripping salt water as held between the fingers,
They are gulped down as a groper,
Blind with huge dull eyes, mumbles weed on rocks,
Till sated, they belch and flop away
In a dribble of towels and flapping thongs.

But in Ostia the small brown Romans
Dived deep into the element,
With the alertness of a gull sighting flake of fish.
Water held as their port in the hands of the sea,
Thus cradled and rocked, they watched
The sad dying of dolphins in nets,
Or the squids cast down on the mosaics.

No wonder they were brothers to the sea,
And saw the huge marriage feast of Neptune
Where nymphs and horses and gods trailed tails,
Sexual, rhythmic and pulsing through water,
Their proudest stance
Was prone or diving down
Into the raptures of the deep,
Where, in bronzed love, these water gods
Laughed ripples of minnows from their mouths.

The Tigers

Quiet! They pad the sleep
Swept streets,
Like inspectors of tombs
Secret, unholy things —
Their strange bodies, prisons
Rippling water.

In the tree whispered night,
Their voices are tiny thunder;
Their eyes, twin torches in
Withdrawn caves;
And their teeth, white Daniels
In flame and red dens.

And behind in pathetic unconcern
The mangled dog
Grins its dead teeth
Imbecilic at the frozen moon.

1970

Writing On

Sigmund Freud wrote on Totem
And Taboo,
Nancy Mitfor wrote on U and
Non U,
Even Lawrence wrote on a
Kangaroo,
But all I ever write on
Is my arse!

1970

Today an Indian Died

Glowing in the embers of college bar drink
While hearing of the Indian's death,
We suffused each other's surviving glory,
With the mock complicity of another staffroom story.

I had seen him but a day
Asleep with age, lonely in his chair,
And my pity aroused, I left him drowse,
For prior words had met with vacant stare.

Lost in his thoughts he shivered in English cold,
Lonely, he slipped away like a sole petrel among gulls,
His dignity come from awkward avoidance.

A shocked quiet held in the pause of thirsty lips,
then the quote of 'Bloody deaths and quick promotions!'
And three triggering Pakistani jokes,
As we slipped back into our private concerns.

Sunderland College Common Room, Sunderland, UK, c. 1970

For Bologna, Yet a Third Time
for James and Donatella

Like a Pasolini bursting through the arcades
I read Bologna afresh —
I, too have wanted to run in and out of the pillars
Shouting streamers of discovery and acceptance
As medieval banners behind me.

Like a Pasolini to be delivered thrice over-
After a respite of milk and brandy and coffee,
To be shot and lie in a shallow ditch.
Did the brother see the brother image
As he too scrabbled to his death, abandoned in a ditch
Chest crushed beyond all hope?

By the horse and the flaunting stone
The homo-erotic made more than heroic,
In amongst the countless photos that indent the wall
Rimmed and rimed in martyr's blood
Brighter, bluer than any tesserae in cupola,
I see now a melancholy that broods down from the hill
Over this labyrinth city,
Sharper than any grappa and as corrosive,
Yet equally liquid pure,
Like a Salò with a dying dictator
Striving in orgy for death's quintessence

Now twice told, Bologna,
And my return before I am old —
Past the burnished glory of Venice
Tarnished in late afternoon,

Decadence drifting from redecorated ceilings
And from grappa to brandy to whisky
To bloodshot eyes and fur filled morning mouth
Such warmth turned to chill
By the sight of a boy lying in a cold doorway
Through that night, and then a rush to a dawn train
As heavy as breakfast in the vaporetto.

And yet, so ill-defined but strong in feeling
Am I to repeat that silent town Casarsa
That in Pasolini's pride and poetic regard
Moved beyond a fire, plague, and Turkish invasion,
Yet had nothing to record
Though its five hundred years were all there
In the silence of work, sufferance, death and prayer.

Perth, 1987
Winner of the inaugural Randolph Stow Literary Award 1987
Published in The West Australian, Saturday 11 July 1987

Venice

'La bella Venezia!'
What's to say of it?
They've all said
That what they say
About Venice
Has been said already —

That every *campo* on the margins
Has a tourist looking at a solitary tourist
Remarking on their own unique singularity
At the other's contradictory expense —

That even to say 'Cats!'
Which are everywhere in Venice
Is to descend into a ghetto of *gatti* —

Each observation is marked in desultory catalogue
Rebarbative and repetitive like Venetian cartography
Where every street, and *fondamente*, and *campo*
Is 'Straight ahead — diretto!'
And there is no getting lost,
Because everyone is lost.

There! I've said it!
And I don't think I am the last!

Hotel Dante, Padova, Italy, 2001
Published in Metior

Not Yet Left India, I Shall Return

Through the little star towns, I drift down the galaxy of Delhi
I watch through the jet's window, along its beam of light,
In a swound with Kishori in Bhawari through earphones.
In a rich melancholy, as with the Peshwar of Parvati
Heartbroken as his mid Empire, newly won, drifts away.
I have come to India, I have never left India.
At the meal's end there is always fennel seed in my teeth.

Outside on the tarmac the long buses run others to Delhi,
But in my transit to Rome, I remember the Calcutta rickshaw
The man running in front of me bearing our shame of man riding
                                                            man;
'Til we scrabbled over rupees: like a tramp engineer firing up steam
My bearer wiping his sweaty brow with an oily rag:
'Til I turn and walk away up hotel stairs,
Away from our guilt as in a blanking dream.

As Sen says that within a fortnight away,
The elegance of Europe's faery towns
and America's prancing pageant pales,
So that he must return to Calcutta's stench, seed bed of all his films
Where stink, slime, sperm, scent
And the monsoon erupts to drown all brown in green.

Now India sleeps, it is one in the Delhi dawning
But my eyes seal.
In Pune a gaffer burns through life to death,
Sinuous Lucifer, filigreeing film with light and shadow.
Intense with night he speaks hour on hour with me as stranger
Then drifts away towards his flaming lonely light.

In late afternoon and the drowsy forest, his quiet hut flares,
As he immolates meditation and self,
Tottering forward in a scream of fiery light.
Symbol, he moves into symbol for his own son to find.
Ram burns for Sita, Sita burns for Ram.

Full of scent and incense, the plane lifts,
The pilot talking past beacon to ride the night for Rome,
But in India a man is burning
And I have not left India, though jets flare the clouds.
With Satjayit, I am before the taba,
Ushers in the raga, I am with Ray
Waiting for the single sound of raindrop hitting dust.

Twenty years before, Bombay was a lovely strand
Beach with boats and nets and crows,
But now from Basu's house, the balcony juts black over iron rock,
Past the morning glory of blooming cacti,
The Bombay beach rots with squatters,
While on the mansion's wall tribal pictures
Slip squat worm gods liquid as the trunk that moves in Ganesh's face

Drifted beyond young rage, India is torn with age.
Parsee towers crumble into dust as kites wheel away
To the dying jungles, melting peaks, drying swamps.
Chariot wheels rust as rickshaws run.
With a man in Pune, India burns.
I have not yet come to India; to India I return.

In transit with Air India, November 1982

At the Fairlawn Hotel, Calcutta

The photo is so green —
Bamboo shafts shade darker than sunstrapped crow,
Pot plants fluoresce bomb blasts of colour,
Bouganvillea spikes the eyeballs with purple and white -
That I cannot give you the deadly stillness,
The sharp bright curiosity, sexual,
In our conversational exchange
In the humid heat of our Calcutta oasis.

Against the humid movement of thighs against thighs,
Saris and dhotis awry, of the city sleepers,
Vulnerable and open on midnight pavements,
In a world coeval, polypping with people along any littoral,
Cancerous, splendid and past words —
Multiple beyond identity —
Our talk is like a sheet drawn across capsized breasts and questing
eyes.

Unlike Pound's scarf; silk, vagrant, and dying on Kensington Park
spikes
Though the smell of fading Empire here is musk amongst gin slings,
And there's still a lot of freight down from Kabul and Kathmandu,
Along with the quinine, the incense sticks and saris -
Calcutta throbs like a distended pudenda just outside.

In the mob on the move
Of Irish girls as wild and tough as boys,
Down from Dacca on furlough
From the Catholic charity hospitals and school,
We sip her whisky from the Duty Free shop.
She has a colour of talking —

A fine drawn face, a page boy's alertness —
That flares and flowers up
Amongst the desultory beers
And drowned downed Johnny Walkers.

In her speaking one saw horses rush on Irish turf,
Past her father's bookies stand and the sordid tips of Dublin,
To the white table cloths 'champers' and sunflower hats,
And longlegged as etchings in smoking rooms,
The top hats and gold tipped canes
Limned yet again in simple barber's shops

Beyond this, she moved into India and worse —
Bangladesh and medicine and dash
Cigarettes and duty free —
Amongst women pregnant and endless dying
Beyond simple meaning.
Like a crushed paste dotted on an ecstasy temple,
Or whitewashed against the teeming mud
To create a comic universal eye,
Cosmic in the sighing drying dust.

No photo can give
Our florid trickle of thigh moving against thigh,
Nor the waiter hiding his tip in the flowers
Away from the manager's eye,
As if rupees would grow like sunspots,
Like blistering film, in the garden's peacock tail.

Lost in our words,
Like a frangipani in water
Her femininity disregards itself
Yet spins in the humid midnight,
And she moves beyond precious sod,
Beyond name, beyond recall
Into no address.

Perth, 1987
First Place, Tom Collins Poetry Prize, 1988

At World's End
for Donald Stuart

To be arranged like this,
All compacted in a poem.
But like your two Chinese sages
At their board,
The discs are ever-moving and in all directions.

A fitful dream of unbelief
Tells here at your world's end and former home
That you are gone
And I am lost in traces and ribbons of memory,
Striding through a field of carnations to your party,
Or watch your hands dancing over buttons
To make sounds and patterns of meaning
Calling up the drama of the world,
Or calling on people to speak to people,
And your curling hair, rakish beard, vagrant smile
Dance like you and the grass in the wind, here now at Land's End.

The church in the fields,
With its window eyes,
Looks over you and your neighbours
And the animals in the field quietly moving and pacing.
Your love is traced in honour here,
Religion has bent itself left and right for you
So it may merge and mingle
With your gospel of the free spirit,
The accepting soul.

A boat has beached in the field
With sheep browsing all around,
And his face a hairy Ulysses,
King Neptune moves into and buffets the wind.

To be arranged like this
All compacted in the ground,
Their loving hands digging, loving feet dancing,
Bringing out the wine from the grapes.

He knows the gypsy road,
He conjures people up as friends all around him,
He backpacks his wisdom on the long car journey
And these hitchhikers are drawn to stand
And share in the words and dance and music.

Of the hundred and more at his grave.
The priest dances with the witch,
Your non-believers are caught in your epiphany,
The Celtic strains are full bodied
In the people of the hamlet.

Like the loveliest child's box
We see flowers, and painted rocks
And charmed metal stars and crescents
And poems on wood,
And they are endlessly appearing and
Disappearing, so they say, down
To the pirates' chest lovingly made
Then laid at your feet
And we who have walked through your fields
Lay red carnations to remember you
Here, as I said, at Land's End.

You are here, but not here,
For I feel your spirit run like red fox
As groundswell, as great songline,
Out from this small earth

Through the fields and over the walls
And through the rocks
To the wild sea,
And you are laughing in the wind,
Your teeth dancing in a smile,
Your beard salting in the waves and spray,
As you sail into the worlds beyond.

Land's End, England, 1999

In This My Native Land

Deputy: Collie Coal Mines

We walked down the shaft of dying time;
Each avoided sleeper a year, and a thousand years,
In this coeval blast of steam and scalding rock.
Pit horses stood silent as sculpture,
Movement seeped like lava in the cells,
And walls wept Calvaries against their crucifying stays.

This guide, older than Cyclops,
With veins thick as honeycombing shafts,
Quarried the darkness with his one eye;
Noted noxious gases in a chiselled script;
Asbsentmindedly like a man forever among horses,
Patted the grab that mantissed its prey;
And bore us to the light — Christopher and king.

Now the town is with his mine
A secret wound that quarries back
Into the catafalque of man and coal.
Men are mazed in this sudden blast
That locks their tunnels;
The gas of change cripples the nerves.

This Sunday, bereft of role,
He watches the open lake of the Muja cut,
Where machines bite like minnows at the exposed coal,
And walks home again.

He is lost in his smallness —
Tall gums watch his steps away from his kingdom.

Harvey, Western Australia, c. 1961

The Dawn is to Come

Storm blast holds morning.
Sun, frustrate, glowers warning.
The trees move colloidal in the wind,
And eye to blanket and curtain
Your hair fronds comfort.
Warmth rises within us,
Phantoms flee our embrace
And our sleeping heads lie face to face.

The winter's sun is up.
Clothes sog wet into grass,
Drip steamily from the lines.
Insects rise in the smoking ladder of sun.
Great blooms flame from the furze;
Our blood stirs,
Fish fret the water
And like a giant the world
Begins its dance.

Guildford, 1973
Second Place in the Tom Collins Poetry Prize

Palmyra – On the Terrace

Perfection and a great unease —
The sun Rousseaus the palm and rubber tree,
Soda and wine in a hexagonal glass to come,
Hockney lies in a big splash on the card table,

Like a gas drift, faintly pattering the banana,
From the line of metal sprinklers on plastic pipes,
A wave of chill dances over the maize and tomatoes
And matches the breeze sudden and cold from the sea.

As I watch the concrete slabs regulate the terrace,
As the Mahawat ash goes white and grey and black
In a crayon smudge at the edge of this page,
And makes this poem sophisticate,
And wonders if the day vanishes in a trance
That might not even be marked,
And wonder when I will begin
To write revolution and relate
To others to hear and know and enjoy and agree.

Should I rise up and spray graffiti,
Instead of this black on yellow paper
With artful and select words and in Parker
Or would I see a white urinal, silver fitting,
Gays flitting delicate wrists beneath hot air driers
And walk back into the unlit bar
And leave my can next to the martini and swizzle,
And drift into the happy hour and rattan of Henry Africa's.

Palmyra, 22 February 1983

Harvey is Holland in the Rain
for Tiel and Anni

Harvey is Holland, in the rain.
Little girls with red hoods buttoning in the winter warmth,
Bobbing the black tar roads like jaunting robins.

Canals etch the earth,
Limn the trees, growing apples,
Turn the sweating mud
For spuds beneath the boots and black Italian hair.

The wind howls the trees.
Houses have taken in their Wellingtons.
The earth comes sudden clean,
And shrubs glisten under the housewife rinse of rain.

I am in Zwijndrecht,
The trains cutting canals into Rotterdam,
Where I drink gins in a steamy bar
In the happy happenstance of the old sailor and his wife.

Those days landlocked in Holland
Because of the endless fog around Bremen,
Daily the taste of witlow and sausage and soup,
And the saunter with the dog in the car to Leyden,
And the ever sense of Holland as cleanness.

Such a sense of minor joy, a steady security.
Even the prostitute wore a fur coat as warmth
On the cold wet street glistening in the rain.

Harvey, Western Australia, c. 1964

Bulldozers Clearing with Chain

The giant wombat snuffled forwards
Through valleys of fern and across the rubbled earth,
Meticulous in its search for food
And about it and under it
The trees sapling thin and seven spear cast high,
Crumpled like reeds in a thunderous flood.

The Caterpillars, German and American,
Stamped and snorted on the Australian soil,
Tumbled the termite hills with their strataed life
Neat as any geologist's hammer,
And left them on display in the long avenues of their force.

Their destruction with the scimitar chain
As severe as any Tartar curse,
As any bomber's instrumental precision,
Searching out all the pockets of resistance,
The unyielding branch crushed like any strongman's arm;
The slashing claw of taloned roots snapped back and blunted.
Humble hawk whose feathers are plucked by children;
Mast strength sunk into the earth's deck,
Snapped beam, all ends up, flotsam for the tidal plough;
All the glorious resurrection recrucified.

c. 1966

White Cat, Where Have You Gone?

Grief has a song,
But to sing it is too long.

You would have known what I felt,
As you slept in grass, hissed past cats,
Ate fish guts and crushed heads left on jetties,
And walked down the river
To the yellowing shores,
And swam whiter than surf
To the great stillness of your death,
Deeper than the sun silk screen of your eyes,
Brighter than the moon razored by clouds,
Harsher than the family's calls and tears,
Their well-placed fears.

While they search
We were there.
I watch the wall —
That is all.

Guildford, Easter Sunday, 1974

Lost in a Durban Dream
for Tom Hoy

Indian music plays morality ragas
Through the vaulting canals of blood
That pulse above and behind his eyes.
He squats, a modern guru
With typewriter cutting his thighs
And pounces on letters
As a hawk, with talons and eyes.
Long lines of satori misspelt,
Dense, struggling to break their own weight,
Flow beyond the carriage's halt
And snap back, shuttle quick on loom,
To leave his growing thought broken
But hidden as fate's thread in Indian rugs.

On the night drive to fetch his wife from Yallingup surf
From his camphor box I read those folded sheets
And the great eternal sea of spirit
Flows through the heat, the high grass and trees
To surround me in its hopeful deceits.

'All the world is energy
         And love and hate its tides
         So that newer Adams, greater surfers
         Into ever knowing can ride,
         Bays where thought moves in man
and man moves hills and skies into complicit fruitfulness,
         And all breaks as white waves on roaring golden sand.'

But the door opens, and back from the sea
She talks of the café, the Swiss chef, and human entropy.

No, energy is not flowing free; it is swirls
Eddies, leaping sunspots boiling metal miles high;
White waves breaking on the reef
Are both hope of landfall and assurance of grief.

Windy Habour, Western Australia, 1973

Island Escape

Wine, long French loaf, camembert, olives, tomato, salami
All could be the names of the bays of my idyll.

The bike leans aslant against the wall,
And slightly stupefied the quokkas snuffle the air,
Reaching upwards for some delight that is not there,
While the salt foam dances across the bitumen from the lakes,
Leaving a trace of white — like the chalk-marks of a children's game.

I try to plan the conquest of this
And all my life in a form of words,
But the day drones and dozes on,
And as I gaze at the paper's dancing white,
And the inconsequential marks on the page,
And away up into the sky and the wisping clouds
All thought dies, and I glaze upon the blue.

Should I see this as some terror of sterility,
Struck barren when the planting season is in train,
Or should I lean back and feel the marrow browning in the bone?

Northbridge, 23 August 1993

Broome Party

Away from the lost glasses
Of forgetful drinkers
In the Broome red grass
Near the cartons with blue labels
And acid Moselle,
Frangipani, flowers white,
Delicate, abandoned.

Fitful as sex, race, history —
An abrupt meeting of bodies and minds —
Our restless cluster
Of two girls, three males
Centres around the black writer,
Wits white sharp, moods brooding dark
In lustre erratic as stale musk.

No matter what the German priests say
About the King Billy plates
They hung around her grandfather's neck,
She's no princess, he taunts the youngster, a Kelly.
Why do they have chains about blacks
In the museum photos,
If it is not to shame us so?

Enjoying serious talk at more sober times
The elder is intrigued,
And offers a quieter drink by the beach,
Waves, clean sand, good talk,
No sex — she's a married woman.

It must not be lost, the writer says,
Sex, trans-race, trans-class
Is the only difference men and women have.
Lose that and we have lost identity.

Irish, new come to the North,
One sees an old condition in sterile complaint
And says, 'Blacks don't know what the Irish know!'
Thinking of a tidal collapse of race,
Between Celts, Romans, Cromwell and Spanish Armada men
Where plated chests and crushing thighs
Made one's enemies, one's blood
To be taken in humour and cheerful self-disregard
She says 'The Irish don't know what we blacks know!'
Then sings ice clear out of the bottomless pit
'This is all we have!'

There is a flare of white bougainvillea
And I dismember an apricot bloom without intention
And apologise for the numb cruelty to her sad eyes,
While her young friend snorts white powder
For breath freshener, smokes a fat lump,
Drinks sour Moselle and is
So bored ……..

We are all bored, all good humour,
All drawn out. I creep to the car
And, to faint music and voices, sleep.
Then we drive home, drunken up the streets,
The girls leave outside a house and,
Will not get back in for the motel
'I'm a married woman!' she says.

With a whiff of the sea,
We cruise back through the town,
In laughter and the day warm night air,
The colonial courthouse caught in tourist flare,
And lights everywhere
Like a twenty four hour bus station in Djakarta.

Prevelly – Chapel for the Bushland Bay

We walk through the fine black sand
and onto the paved terrace of the church
and see all Prevelly, bay and chalet and struggling bush
and lolling lawn all spread before us
and the heavenly host of the sun
dancing somewhere off and down to the horizon.

Then we turn the key
Into the whiteness of that wall
And move into the church
With its baptismal font of blackboy butt
A crude but native thing
In this moment from the Greek and Cretan waters
Of a world war past.

In a mutual pleasure, two of us spell out a schoolboy Greek
 on the ikons as donated gifts
and see two archangels hovering in the corners
and a mother forever brooding , holding her Son
as a dark black eagle would hold the world at bay above its young.

There is a coolness half suspect in the new warming spring,
And the ornaments hang in a token aluminium,
Until the patrons of the year and the hundred year,
Turn them into gold or silver and red flamed crystal.

The visitor's book margins its last comment
Into a word and far less short of this poem.

Still the names, every one in three
Ring redolent of Greece and Crete,
And one can sense a sort of daily pilgrimage
With the four hour drive from Perth,
Whether it be the anxious love that marks the Hellenic god,
In its every manifestation in this land of banksia and tuart,
Or the assurance to the visitor that this is not Ultima Thule,
But a new colony over seas
Like the Greek city Gallipoli in Italy,
But half a world away.

Ouside the bush burns and runs
An incense across the low bundled shrubs.

Later we drift into the barbarity of Gracetown,
Its townscape a shattered heartless clutter of shacks
And nondescript houses and no church,
And we remark how in Europe the deep forests,
Long riverways, channels and even windblasted heaths,
Are marked into meaning within every hour's walk,
By a hut, a habiliment or even a cathedral,
And maybe this is what the Greeks miss here
In the dense karri, the empty limestone,
the whale – rocks of the beach,
so that this vestige chapel reassures them,
and in turn is reassured by them.

Northbridge, 7 November 1993

For Juniper

As one newly emerging in the expanding, exploding discovery of art,
I had interviewed Juniper one of our three best -
Even then, fifty years ago, close to classic
And already suspended in Swanland's gallery,
For us to revere until this year and beyond.

And all I remembered of that late sunblast afternoon,
Was myself skipping, stumbling or was it sliding?
In a criss-cross fashion
Down a steep Darlington hill,
Totally primed, sublimed on Bob's White Burgundy —
Like him, considered the State's best.

Re-entered into that afternoon, by his sudden passing,
I can only think of a sun shower,
Compacting rich red earth, and bringing granite and gravel, and quartz
Into bright patinas of small indents of water,
All on an ever diffusing canvas from rich oil to fading pastel,
With a feathering carpet of dried and falling leaves
Cast against the great Kalgoorlie serpent pipe,
Buckled windmills and sliding wooden mine heads,
Making all in its half moistness, half dry
The red, the dust a gentle canvas of patterning delight.

And now in a flash it is all past,
But I will remember until I too pass,
The searing sunblast,
The cooling sweet smelling sunshower
That was Juniper
For me that long gone afternoon and ever now.

Mt Lawley, 31 December 2012

We Live in an Iron Age

Rolling Left the Seaman Lies on Shallow Reef

Rolling left the seaman lies on shallow reef,
On the right the deeps fall away beyond belief
And in that moment born the human race views earth.

Women lost in warmth of milk
And napkinned shit,
Hold the world away,
While husband hunters battle mammoths
And bring home flesh on the harpbone of tusk.

Children are held away
From water, fire, earth, spider in the cave.
They escape,
And taunt the adder with a stick
And weave stars in cat cradles,
So they can entrap the universe
In the wells of their hollowed out canoes.

Women breed again and again
Up the phallused furrows to the sky,
Ears of wheat groan heavier than wombs,
Egyptian priests clerk their granaries to pyramiding tombs.

Viaducts, acqueducts, bridges, roads and tracks of steel -
Trade through sail and timber to steam and steel spans -
All breed cities, factories that rise and fall
As empires that hammer metals into meaning,
Cereals and stock buckling to elemental drought and harvest.

1963

Car in the Rain

Metal, dare I say it again, cocoon

With its own warmth, sound and antennae,
Wipers brushing away silken rain,
It envelops me,
To carry me along the glistening road
To home again,
With its own warmth, sound and antennae,
Newspapers bringing in the flaring world,
To drive me along the glinting road
To work again.

Guildford, 11 June 1973

Assassination

By the Capitol,
The banners hung in starch.
Above our shining heads,
The evening sun was yet to set.

Around us, the home-goers stood on the streets
And watched a finer show
Than their turkey at home and CBS NEWS,
As police bikes tilted in front of us,
Revving like thunder!

We were destiny,
And arm over folded arm
We would overcome.
And every falling foot
Would be our drumbeat.

Our eyes were bright
To find the running lanes of fire.

Up ahead, so far we couldn't see
Our leader lay dead.
Ambulances carved in and out of us
Like fluting sharks.
The drums did not sound.

We stood waiting in the dark.

WAIT, Bentley, 1973

Towards Poetic Journalism

Journalism —
To serve the day,
Everyone's a five minute
Was a five minute
Fucking
celebrity.
Calypsoes cut the day
In couplets
Calypsoes collapse and crumple
Day tickets to
Everywhere.

How cheap is a day?
       Three meals,
              An evacuation,
                     An ejection.

All in a day.
Louie the cripple
Wrote 'Shit!' in the loo.

Perth now,
Nookenbah another entry
In Court's diary of stocks and shares
By St. George's
Sermons drenched the air,
       By St. George's
       I sat down and wept

By St. George's
Palsy white conscience crept
By St. George's
Compassion slept.

1980

New Paint and Old Canavs

While the cynics still slept,
Vision oozed from their pores,
The others came, small pageant from the house
To the morning surf rolling white,
The dawn sun gilding the dunes.

Swirling cape, he strode, floated ahead,
White bags of lime held, as dancers do, at arm's length.
The others, moving to the beat of the rising sun,
The still crashing surf,
Followed their belief in him to ceremony.

Fisher, he cast his painting to the sea,
So large that its fluttering mapped the waves,
Swished away as ghosting mantra towards India.
Maiden; freshly dressed for the new day,
Its colour held fast, he swam it back to shore
Trailing its coolness about him.

As he sank devotion to its knees,
He traced its colour with folds of sand,
Trying to sculpt it to lignum,
But vigour oozed away in flaccid lime,
His sculpture melting sand into drying amoeba.

The sun was hot;
The blankness bored them.
And as he rose fervid prince from his sallow bed,
The harem turned

And watched the sea turn lead.

Lost in the great romance, Ego,
Centerpiece in his own ageing crown,
He cannot see that no new spell
Will ever lure the young again to his dance.

Published in Soundings, Fremantle Centre Press, 1976

Anaias

Anaias
Ties his craft to the wharf with a rope of sand
Anchors down with the minnow breakers.

Romance is turgid in the muddy river
Detachment changes it to level broad expanse
Both are wrong
Beneath the surface rocks are crushed.

When the leaders clash, the tribe agitates
Down through the chain of speakers,
Only grandmother moves and fills the pots with beer,
She works and removes her fears.

When the young blade settles it
In a sudden dagger thrust,
His head benumbed by argument,
The tribe swirls, moves, splits
And the old lady moves to the bigger group
Making herself useful, beginning the little tasks.

7 June 1978

Rivers of Piss

Starker than the nearby beach —
The water shallow and no dunes, no trees —
The yard holds six hundred men
The dull burn of the sun and two buckets of shit

Moorhouse exasperated by his two ever cheating guides
At their final request teaches them English;
"We like to work for you,
but remember this - I am a cunning little shit
and he is a long streak of piss! Trust us!"
But such humour has no meaning here.

To squat above the bucket like a woman;
To moon in full view;
To hold dignity in saunter, strut,
And casual curve of urine shining in the air,
As if it were all mere afterthought;
A flourish to end the walk.

Ever in the theatre of each other's gaze,
Eyes locked, cast aslant, or searching the shadows
From the other's feet,
Or mad-looking eyeball, white head lolling
Back into the circle of the sun.

Patterns of piss that miss or rim the edge,
Scatter shot plunge of melting into steaming sand.

Clear yellow and memories of drenched cider,

Lingering asparagus.

The rush of blood from the balls and the beating,
The legs akimbo as the young cadet
Who faints in the sun, nicks his chin
With the bayonet, and shudders
Mapping the front of his trousers in shame.
The beating lingers on.

The hint of sperm, white flecks of snow,
From a vague trance memory of the restless hand,
The penis head hooded or red domed
With its own spider web of restless night,
And in such exposure the vagaries of a romance.

Genet in audacity folding paper over his member
And sending the smears to his lover two cells up.

Hodge and the anecdote of why men
Find it hard to piss alongside others,
From the fear shaped in the Biblical text,
"Go ye among them and disregard them that squat,
and find all who piss against the wall,
and dash their brains out!"

The wall is a circling convent yard of neutered men,
A harem of all types and conditions,
An endless cartography in official catalogue
Of measured days to sit stupid in the sun.
A long line of men, a long line of piss
Standing one after the other to address the buckets.

Outside these walls the Swan
Straggles like a long river of piss
To the sea.

Note: Inspired by notes taken by Murdoch academic Tony Miller from the 1988 Draft Conservation and Management Plan for Fremantle Prison pp. 20/22.

To Hell with the Quotidian

The quotidian makes everyday predictable, manageable,
Boring but ensuringly comfortable
The tablets counted and taken
A good night's sleep
The bins wheeled out for the weekly take-up
The two papers delivered
The kettle filled and the tap tightly turned off,
The kitchen gas in flame and boiling morning coffee,
The animals fed and all in order,
The car locked and fuelled and ready to go,
The weekly hydro with its health restoring exercise.
This to be repeated week in week out
Year in year out.

My sister died at 9.15 pm.
Somewhere between the TV miniseries of *Banshee* and *Midwives*
My sister died at 9.15
Not at five in the afternoon like the matador in the glory of the dying sun
But on a sparse hospital bed arched for comfort
With a regulatory pump near her chest
With just the right mixtures to keep her in comfort
And paced alongside the six days without food
And comatose, eyes shut, losing contact with us
Her arm occasionally reaching out for a cigarette,
Hovering and falling away, so was her dream,
Not of people but the endlessly soothing of nicotine,
Her lips pursed not to kiss kith and kin,
But to hold to one long final embrace of the tobacco tube.
In mid-episode I rose to the phone knowing she had gone,

So grateful for her release, but part annoyed at the visual break,
Then smiling, because if she were watching with me she would see
Nurses moving on a diurnal round bringing life into the world
Just as she, as nurse,
had brought comfort and humour through the wards.

The swirl, the twirl, the whirl of it all
That day the quotidian went askew, akimbo

A restless night because the painkilling tablet not taken, forgotten.
Up at three then four so to hell with sleep
The overfull bin wheel - out forgotten and now another week to wait
The newspapers - only the one delivered
 but with the arts section missing
The water tap endlessly dripping then stopped for $275
all for a damaged 50c washer
The gas stove leaking,
The dead rat beside the drain to be shovelled and taken from sight
The car rifled with documents left
The hydro closed down,

My sister died at 9.15
Extreme unction recited and exhausted.

Oh, to hell with the quotidian.

Mt Lawley, 18 January 2014

For My Young Wife

'It's just arithmetic. That's what it comes down to. Boughton has married four or five of his children. Baptized a dozen grandchildren by now. And maybe I'll teach this fellow to tie his shoelaces. The years of a man's life are threescore years and ten, give or take. That's how it is...I feel like Moses on the mountain, looking out on the life he will never have. Then I think of the life I do have. And that starts me thinking of the life I won't have. All that beautiful life...I guess I'm pretty hard to please.'

LILA by Marilynne Robinson

You are my Lila in Gilead
And I am your Preacher
We have taken each other in for many years now
And soon I will have to depart
Leaving you to your years without me
As with those years for both of us before we met.

In those years when we were yet to meet,
We married and coupled and domesticated,
Travelled and finally fell out, partnered no more.
The past has left its integuments and recriminations
But was and is rarely drawn upon,
Leaving a fairly clean board to write on anew.

Inshallah! Buddhist calm, I have come to move
beyond the passion of jealousy and envy,
until now, when I speculate on your possible companions to be,
Such a companion, my long time friend
Might prove suitable when I have gone
But I found I envied him his extra years
Left for him to share if need be,
Just as you climbed the path to view Mount Macedon

While I book in hand retreated to my rest in the car,
All exercise spent, except to wonder about
That Hanging Rock and its challenge,
The picnicking girls laughing, haphazardly climbing,
Playfully holding hands and then vanishing, into endless silence.
Grey nomad that he is now and with friends
Throughout the world,
Maybe he could cease wandering and properly couple.
That emotion I felt part flattering, part pure speculation,
Part disabling, swelling up, but is now gone,
And I am back in a twilit calm.

Or will it lead to a loneliness that makes living sterile,
Constantly tired forever seeking sleep
Wondering if you were taken in the night
It would be a blessed relief,
For there seems that there is nothing more ,
All the endlessly same,
Day in, night out.

Or will you be well placed in solitude, family centred but apart,
happily responding to the world in your unique personal creativity
idiosyncratic and unremarkable as it may be,
but a long life, a happy life, possibly fuller than ours?

Mount Lawley, January 2015

Acknowledgements

As always there are teachers who fanned the sparks such as Gerald Hare, that gentlemanly scholar and commando, whom we all admired for his courtesy and individual attention to each and everyone of us. Then Norm Kirkham with his great comic readings of Damon Runyon and Stephen Leacock, and his goading of me from my tawdry imitations of robust modern American fiction, into assaying a poem or two as the most demanding and elegant of literary forms, leading to an endpiece in our final year annual.

Claremont Training College saw me writing for both the *Centaur* and *Chiron* under the editorship of Bill Grono and Roger Dixon with lots of helpful advice and in turn editorship in the following year. This allowed Bob Biggins to award me the Bertha Houghton Prize and the key to the glass cabinet in which lay *Ulysses*. Bill has proved a lifelong friend and as a saintly sinner to lure me hitch hiking across Australia to King's Cross just before I entered National Service. I hereby apologise for not notifying him about submitting without acknowledgement of earlier publication a poem to the *Bulletin*.

As to my teaching career J.P. Molony, my headmaster of the Perenjori 3 teacher primary was a kind supportive mentor, who shaped me into a caring teacher with his wisdom, and my admiration of him as a family man, and a wartime hero of the famous Pathfinder squadrons. Brother Fogarty the Highgate Christian Brother, who allowed me to control a bracing class of some 80 eleven year olds and then to teach our Leaving Class the poetry of Gerald Manley Hopkins, and to conduct a verse choir for the school graduation. He gave a prize for the tryptich art that my startlingly talented juvenile artists generated as a taste of the Catholic cultural heritage. Onto Christchurch then, and my generous appointment to Senior Master by Peter Moyes for a year prior to leaving for England, and ultimately Sunderland College of Education with John Christopher as a person quixotically hopeful of my becoming a linguist. My return to WAIT and the faith and encouragement of Tony Hoffman in my ability to forge new courses in Film and Television and Creative Writing. A golden chain that allowed me to allow my students to teach me as much as themselves by taking up the creative challenge of working on projects of their own individual and personal choice.

Onto our own literary scene with its committee membership of the FAW with people like Bert Vickers, Oz Watson, Donald Stuart and Mary Durack and the post meeting round of multiple sherries. Throughout my writing career Dorothy Hewett and Merv Lilley kept a helpful and watchful eye on my output. My own generational thrust with Griffith Watkins, captain of a motley crew and a personal mentor, and the Leederville Tech next generation with Lee Knowles and Andrew Burke marked poetic endeavours in magazines, café and theatrical readings. People like Peter Bibby, the 'wunderkind' of our generation who has gone on to chair FAWWA.

Griff and one of my dearest friends Malcolm Levine and myself launched *Poets 3* in the Skinner Galleries as a purely local poetry initiative. Over the following years it reached *Poets 9* with readings at the Dolphin. Shortly after Glen Phillips organized *Poetry in Motion* with Alan Alexander and Shane McCauley and they even went international in Singapore. My own students at WAIT made waves with the humorously named Spanish Onion under John Catlin and Phil Collier and Donna Devine. And on and on, that vein of poetry maintained by the many group transformations until our own *WA Poetry Inc.* festivals now in their tenth year and a State cultural bedrock.

In England I published my first and only small book *Scapes* and owe that to the remarkable arts lab *Coelfrith Press* in Sunderland. My other very dear friend John Daniel, academic and celebrated Devon poet forged a lifelong friendship with mutual encouragement.

To this current endeavour with the initial selection by Chris Palazzolo and the encouragement of Nathan Hondros, and the supportive typing of Daphne Farsalis in its speculative early stages. A preliminary edit by Glen Phillips has proved most helpful.

This descent into a potted literary history is merely to emphasise what I have already discussed — the making and sharing of poetry with others whatever it be, whomever with, and however defined.

Lastly and primarily, the support of my family throughout all the triumphs and crises of my life, who have tolerated perhaps an over commitment to public arts and given me the space to create and travel in search of inspirational experience. Where would our identity and our existence be without family?

Peter Wadds Jeffery, OAM
2015

Printed in Australia
AUOC02n1612151215
272488AU00003B/3/P

9 780987 482167